napa bulletin 9

Anthropology and Management Consulting: Forging a New Alliance

Maureen J. Giovannini and Lynne M. H. Rosansky

National Association for the Practice of Anthropology
A Unit of the American Anthropological Association

NAPA Bulletins are occasional publications of the National Association for the Practice of Anthropology, a Unit of the American Anthropological Association.

Ralph J. Bishop and Pamela Amoss
General Editors

Library of Congress Cataloging-in-Publication Data

Giovannini, Maureen J.
Anthropology and management consulting : forging a new alliance / Maureen J. Giovannini and Lynne M. H. Rosansky.
p. cm. — (NAPA bulletin ; 9)
Includes bibliographical references.
ISBN 0-913167-37-1
1. Applied anthropology. 2. Business consultants. 3. Corporate culture. I. Rosansky, Lynne M. H. II. Title. III. Series.
GN397.5.G56 1990
658.46—dc20 90-30344
CIP

ISBN 0-913167-37-1

Contents

Introduction

Over the last century, anthropologists have created a discipline to make sense out of human behavior through the culture concept, a holistic analytical approach, and empirical research. Although anthropological concepts have been defined largely in academia, the discipline has always had "applied" practitioners working in areas like health care, education, business and industry (Chambers 1985; Eddy and Partridge 1978; Holzberg and Giovannini 1981). These practitioners have demonstrated time and again that an anthropological perspective has a great deal to offer the wider world.

In this monograph we focus on the practice of anthropology in one part of that world—the domain of management consulting and the business issues that consultants address. At first glance, the two professions—anthropology and management consulting—may appear highly dissimilar. But a closer look reveals many points of common interest. For example, like anthropologists, management consultants attempt to make sense out of human behavior as they address the "people" dimensions of doing business. Hence, there is an opportunity for a valuable exchange between anthropologists and management consultants. To some extent this is already taking place. Anthropologists are working as consultants and many consultants are using an anthropological perspective—perhaps without knowing it. To further this exchange, we focus on the contributions that anthropology can make to management consulting and business.

Our discussion is directed primarily toward anthropologists interested in the field of management consulting. But the information we present should also be useful to practicing consultants who want to adopt an anthropological perspective and to managers themselves as they attempt to diagnose and solve business problems and take advantage of new opportunities.

In the chapters that follow, we give an overview of the wider business environment, including the challenges that managers face today. We then describe the management consulting industry and the consulting process. The next chapter looks at the contributions that anthropology can make to management consulting and business, illustrating these through case examples. This is followed by a discussion of how anthropologists can become management consultants. Finally, we conclude by summarizing the benefits that result from exchanges between anthropology and management consulting in practice, research, and teaching. It is our hope that this discussion will stimulate ongoing dialogue between anthropologists and management consultants and increase the practical applications of anthropology in the business arena.

The Background

Environmental Changes and Challenges

The almost exponential rate of change in the contemporary business world challenges business leaders in many ways.[1] The survival of a business depends on management's ability to adjust to change. Anthropology can help consultants and their clients respond successfully to five major trends that will shape the way we all live and work in the future.

1. *Increasing Globalization* The world will continue to shrink as companies are pressed into thinking about their products, customers, production processes, and supply sources in terms of a global market and a global economy. Communication improvements will contribute to making our world smaller. Products will be available more quickly around the world and customer bases will continue to broaden. Managers will have to learn to adapt quickly to all kinds of changing circumstances—be they product, people, markets or suppliers (*Business Week,* 16 October 1989; *Fortune,* 3 July 1989; Haynes 1989).

2. *Demographic Trends* The aging of the baby boom generation will bring changes to the work force. In the United States there will be a significant dip in the number of people available for entry-level jobs. This will mean that companies will have to select new recruits from a more diverse pool of applicants. Entry-level jobs will be filled with more women, blacks, Hispanics and Asians than ever before. As more women enter the work force, childcare issues will become more important. Competition between companies for the best and brightest will increase. Correspondingly, as the experienced work force ages, companies will have to offer more education, training, and other incentives to attract and keep employees (Wilhite 1989).

3. *Social Issues* In the 1990s there will be many social issues for business leaders to contend with—the changing health needs of workers, addictions to alcohol and illegal drugs, mandatory versus elective retirement. But analysts expect that the environment will be the issue of greatest concern. For example, continuing overuse will cause water shortages. Sewer and waste disposal issues will intensify due to demands on existing systems. Global warming will exacerbate water shortages. As we move into the 1990s, there is likely to be more legislative action and demand for accountability for these and other problems. As society increasingly holds

business responsible for maintaining a clean environment, the costs of clean up and prevention will be felt by everyone—producers and consumers alike.

4. *Technological Innovation* Innovations in technology will continue to change the way both large and small companies operate. Information technology will alter the way coworkers communicate and interact. Today, for example, many employees communicate via voice mail as well as electronic mail. These changes involve not only the introduction of new technology but have influenced social relations as well (Schein 1985).[2] Eventually, technological advances will affect the entire business structure, including how customers and suppliers conduct business nationally and internationally.

5. *Organizational Change* Due in part to the information flows and in part in response to competitive pressures, organizations will become flatter. There will be fewer mid-level managers and existing managers will supervise a larger staff. At the same time, organizations will become more flexible—for example, there may be more people working at home. Globalization and a shrinking labor pool will increase the need for these kinds of alternatives within an organization.

What Is Management?

"Just what is a manager, anyway? The standard response to this question is that a manager is a person who gets things done through other people. In the broadest sense of the term, a manager is responsible for carrying out the activities needed to reach organizational goals" (Taylor and Rosansky 1988:9). The related term, management, is used either to refer to the people in an organization who are doing the managing or the set of behaviors people perform while managing. Our focus here is with the behavioral aspect of management—the activity that managers engage in as they get things done by others. Viewed this way, management has been practiced since Moses when Jethro advised him to "appoint rulers of thousands, of hundreds, of fifties, and of tens" (Exodus XVIII:21) as a way to reduce the burden on himself. There are many other examples throughout the history and prehistory of management in practice.

It is only since the Industrial Revolution that management has been identified as an area for "scientific" study. Frederick Taylor (1856–1915) is known as the father of scientific management because he developed certain principles that he believed would increase productivity. A Frenchman, Henri Fayol (1841–1925) observed the management of organizations and identified four basic functions of management: (1) planning, (2) organizing, (3) directing, and (4) controlling (Fayol 1949).[3]

Looking more closely at what managers really do, Mintzberg concluded "these four words, which have dominated management vocabulary since the French industrialist Henri Fayol first introduced them in 1916, tell us little about what managers actually do. At best, they indicate some vague objectives managers have when they work" (1984:284–289). Mintzberg found that management actually means an ability to integrate ten roles: figurehead, leader, liaison, monitor, disseminator, spokesmen, entrepreneur, disturbance handler, resource allocator and negotiator.

We associate "management" with "business" because the business community has formalized the term and the roles within their organizations. But management is not an activity confined to the business world. Rather, it is practiced every day in every setting. Management is found in government and nonprofit institutions such as hospitals, schools and universities. It is also practiced in households and among social and recreational groups. Management consultants work with managers in these and other settings to help them do their jobs more effectively. As we describe below, there are many types of management consultants, just as there are many types of managers.

New Challenges for Managers

Although the basic roles of managers will probably remain constant as managers move into the 1990s, the *contexts* in which such roles take place will be new. Specifically, the increasing globalization of business and diversification of the U.S. work force will force U.S. managers to move beyond their traditional management styles and the cultural assumptions underlying them.

As business becomes more global, managers will have to learn the realities of recruiting, developing, and rewarding foreign nationals in overseas offices. They will also have to become adept at producing and marketing in new cultures, taking advantage of local resources and customs. All of this involves developing a sensitivity to cultural differences, understanding diverse and sometimes conflicting social forces, and operating in unfamiliar and uncomfortable organizational settings. As the following example illustrates, once this sensitivity is acquired, new strategies can be devised that contribute to successful cross-national business dealings (Adler 1986; Phatak 1989).

Many U.S. companies accuse their Japanese competitors of unfair trade practices, complaining that Japanese markets are "closed" to U.S. business. A closer look at some of these situations reveals that U.S. businessmen seldom understand the Japanese distribution system. In the United States, business subscribes to the ideal of a "free" market, in which all producers compete freely with each other and the "customer" chooses on the basis of quality, price and availability. The Japanese, on the other hand, value stable business relationships (a special class of social relationships) more than a "free" market. Therefore, Japanese businesses develop and nurture an important relationship between customer and supplier. It would be an affront to this relationship for the Japanese customer to suddenly switch suppliers. However, American businesses and customers do this frequently, with no "dishonor" or "shame" to consider. Some American companies have capitalized on these Japanese patterns by forming joint ventures with Japanese companies. In these joint ventures, the American partner supplies the products, while the Japanese partner is responsible for marketing and distribution. If the Japanese partner is chosen well, there will be a history of relationships with customers, which can be used in distributing the American product (Prestowitz 1988).

Even those managers whose companies are primarily U.S.-based will find that the growing diversity of the work force will require them to direct and motivate employees across ethnic, gender, and age boundaries. Already 53% of the current U.S. work force is made up of minorities, women, and people from other countries, who, by the year 2,000, will constitute over 80% of our domestic work force (Hanamura 1989).

When managers are unaware of subcultural differences in perceptions and values, real problems can result. For example, U.S. managers are advised to use a system of rewards, which includes some public recognition and praise, in order to encourage employees to work efficiently and carefully. While public praise and acknowledgment motivate many employees, it may be a disincentive for others. To illustrate, a Native American, whose culture frowns upon competition, may be excessively embarrassed at being singled out for praise in front of peers. The manager's motivation technique may backfire and make such a worker self-conscious and paralyzed.[4]

Fortunately, some U.S. companies and their leaders are already recognizing the importance of managing diversity. For example, Digital Corporation has incorporated the value of diversity into its philosophy as well as its activities (*Boston Globe*, 21 August 1988). Among other things, Digital has developed a corporate training program designed to give managers intercultural awareness and communication skills. This goes far beyond acknowledging the need to *tolerate* differences to emphasize the *real benefits* that a diverse work force can bring to a company—such as multiple perspectives on business problems and opportunities. Recognizing and developing the potential benefits of heterogenity will be particularly important for many companies whose customer base, both nationally and internationally, is also becoming increasingly diverse (Terpstra and David 1985).

Globalization and internal diversity are just two of the issues that U.S. managers will have to address as they move into the 1990s. With change occurring on all fronts, the multiple roles that Mintzberg (1984) says are part of the job of managing will become even more complex. To deal with the increasing complexity, managers will, of course, rely on internal resources. For example, most large companies have a staff of corporate human resource professionals to recruit, select, hire, train, and develop employees. But in many cases, the demands may overwhelm the existing staff. In these cases, companies will probably seek outside help from management consultants. We suggest that the merger of anthropology with management consulting can benefit business leaders by developing new and creative ways to approach these challenges. Before looking more closely at this merger, let us briefly examine what management consulting is all about.

The Field of Management Consulting

Management Consulting as an Industry

Management consultants work on a contract basis with practicing managers to solve work-related problems. Over the past few decades, an industry has evolved around the activities of management consultants that today books approximately 13 billion dollars of sales worldwide. Of this, 10 billion are sales in the United States. Industry growth rates vary around the world—from 14% per year in the United States to 30% per year in the Pacific Basin and 10% in Europe.[5]

Two major trends in particular are responsible for much of this increased business for consultants: globalization (discussed earlier) and downsizing. The first—globalization and the shrinking world—has meant a boom in the use of information systems for communications within and between countries. Concomitant with this boom, conflicts have developed over who should use and have access to information and how it will be incorporated into the business. The second trend—downsizing—has taken place primarily in American companies as they "trim the fat" by reducing some of the layers of middle managers. Both the planning and implementation of downsizing are difficult, so businesses often call in outside consultants to assist. This may include developing programs to help displaced employees find other work. Some consultants also work with companies to assist them in the reorganization effort, either to become more efficient or to meet the needs of a changing market. As we move into the 1990s, the management consulting industry is expected to continue its growth in response to these and other demands.

Types of Consultants/Consulting Firms

Competition and demand have worked together to stimulate differentiation among consulting services. In some ways, management consultants are like doctors. There are general practitioners along with an increasing number of specialists. Like doctors, some consultants practice independently while others are employed by formal institutions—in this case, consulting firms. Many of these firms occupy specialized niches in the industry and restrict themselves to a limited range of problems. Other firms have a broader base and have built up national reputations much like large medical centers.

Today, some larger management consulting firms, such as the Boston Consulting Group and McKinsey and Company, specialize in the analysis and diagnosis of strategic business problems. Their consultants need to understand the client's industry, the environment in which it operates, and corresponding competitive dynamics. Other consulting firms—for example, Developmental Dimensions Inc. and Forum Corp.—specialize in the practice of management. They develop training programs to help businesses provide their managers with needed skills in the areas of negotiation, communication, and improving morale and productivity of the work force. There are also many firms, large and small, that focus on narrow technical issues such as a specialized type of information processing or accounting system. And, finally, the functional domains of business, marketing, finance, human resources, operations and accounting, have each spawned consulting services with specialized knowledge and expertise. These consultants and consulting firms focus on analyzing problems and planning solutions from a *content* perspective. They are usually specialists in a particular industry or business function who help managers with particular aspects of a business challenge, such as whether or not to expand into a new market, how to position a new product, or whether to adopt a new technology.

In addition to those affiliated with consulting firms, there are many consultants who work independently. Although they are an important factor in the industry, there is no aggregate data available on them so that the industry statistics do not include their contributions. Most independent consultants develop their client base from informal contacts and referrals from colleagues. This frequently centers around business school faculty who are often engaged in independent consulting. Some professional associations, such as the American Society for Training and Development (ASTD), the National Organizational Development Network, and the Management Consulting Division of the Academy of Management serve as meeting grounds for independent consultants. These associations have regular annual meetings and many have regional groups that meet more regularly. ASTD, for example, has annual meetings that draw close to 20,000 people. Local meetings are usually smaller, providing more opportunity to meet and talk with individuals. Professional meetings often sponsor an outside speaker to discuss topics of interest to members.

Clearly, the management consulting industry spans many categories. In this bulletin, we focus on the subset of management consultants, both independent and company-based, who help their clients deal with the *human* dimensions of doing business. This includes, but is not limited to, strategic planning and implementation, marketing research, human resource and organizational development.[6] These types of consultants and their clients can most benefit from an anthropological perspective. Moreover, consulting firms specializing in these areas are likely to be most receptive to anthropological concepts and skills as useful additions to the consulting "tool box" (J. C. Louis 1985; Zemke 1989).

Why Hire a Consultant?

When laypersons talk about management consulting, they often ask these questions: Why do businesses use consultants? Don't business people know their own problems? Why would they need an outsider? Managers hire external consultants for three reasons.

1. *Lack of Internal Expertise or Resources* There may be a lack of perceived or real internal expertise to deal with specific problems—for example, investigating the causes for high employee turnover and devising workable solutions. Even if the internal expertise exists, staff can carry such a heavy workload that an external consultant is hired to get the job done. Or, managers may need a fresh and unbiased point of view on an issue—such as entering a new market, reorganizing, or acquiring a new company.

2. *Lack of Credibility in Proposing Novel Solutions* Even when clients are intimately aware of their organization's issues, consultants can help other individuals in the client company recognize them. Consultants have some initial credibility because of their status as outside experts. Members of the organization may be able to hear the message delivered by consultants when they would ignore it from insiders. Consultants frequently are able to highlight organizational issues and pinpoint particular problems because they do not have as much personal stake in the outcome of any particular decision.

3. *Need for Planning and Implementation Assistance* Having an outsider articulate organizational problems raises the level of consciousness and creates a sense of urgency that will stimulate active responses. Moreover, an outside perspective on the internal workings of a business can be a valuable planning tool for future action, or for implementing immediate changes. Many consultants consider themselves change agents and have frequently played an important role in stimulating organizational improvements.

The Consulting Process

The consulting process can be divided into several chronological phases: entry and contracting; data collection and diagnosis; feedback and the decision to act; implementation; extension/recycle/termination (Block 1981). In this chapter we address some key aspects of that process.

Initial Stages

The consulting process begins when a client actively seeks a consultant, or a consultant creates an opportunity to serve a client. The initial stage of a consulting project is devoted to defining the problem. Clients have varied interpretations of their own problems. In some instances, those who seek a consulting relationship know they have a problem and want help understanding its causes and solving it. For example, the director of an overseas travel business was leaving on a trip to meet with his tour leaders. The company had had a rough year: profits were down; customers were unhappy; equipment and supplies were badly kept; employees were disgruntled and unhappy. The director knew that employee morale was low and customer service poor. He sought a consultant's help to determine the causes and suggest ways to improve the situation.

In other cases, clients understand their problem, but they have come up with the wrong solution—one that they want the consultant to help implement. To illustrate, a large manufacturing company knew they had problems with performance appraisals. Managers were not giving proper feedback and subordinates were not clear about what they were supposed to be doing. The company assumed that the solution involved putting managers through performance management training and hired a consultant to help them implement this. However, the consultant soon discovered that the solution lay not in training but in revising their performance evaluation form. Unfortunately, the evaluation form had been "inherited" from the former Director of Human Resources, who had since become the CEO. The form was written in stone and, for political reasons, could not be changed. In this situation, there was little that the consultant could do to help.

In some cases, clients may have misdiagnosed the problem altogether. For example, a large metropolitan hospital requested outside help designing and implementing a performance management system to enhance efficiency. In the process of interviewing managers, consultants discovered that there were rules and regulations that drove individuals to "go around the system" to get something done, albeit inefficiently. The real problem was not performance management but cumbersome and impractical operating systems.

The assumptions clients have about their problems and solutions may not be immediately apparent. Therefore, consultants should engage in some clarification of the problem *before* committing to a contract. Even when clients are mistaken about problems and solutions, it is usually possible to turn this around. Indeed, an important part of the consultant's role is to help clients frame problems, possible causes, and viable solutions. But when the client has a closed mind, the working relationship may be very difficult. These are situations that the consultant must examine very carefully to determine if it will be possible to help the client or if the appropriate action is to disengage.

Some Pitfalls to Avoid

Consultants should be aware of other possible pitfalls. While a client organization may genuinely need a consultant's assistance, there is risk for the consultant when the decision to bring in an outsider is primarily a political one—for example, when the consultant is hired to address a controversial and volatile issue that insiders are divided over or reluctant to tackle. In this situation, if things go wrong, the consultant may become the scapegoat. Even when consultants are not blamed, internal political battles can significantly affect the fate of their recommendations, as the following case illustrates.

A large financial services institution signed on a team of consultants to review, analyze and assess the performance of the information services department. The consulting team interviewed a range of individuals, including people who used the services of the department as well as members of the department itself. The business had been decentralizing. Thus, many of the services offered by the information services department could be done in the field on personal computers or at workstations. There was disagreement among the senior managers about what should be done with the department. One group wanted the department trimmed, while another wanted to refocus it. The consultants were hired by one senior manager involved in the controversy who lost his political battle and left the organization. The consultants provided a good analysis of the situation in the information services department and had good suggestions for improvement. But their work was never used for any development or change because the consultants and their recommendations were associated with the "loser."

This example raises an important question: When should a consultant (or consulting firm) walk away from a potential consulting assignment? Although there are no hard and fast rules, we can offer some general guidelines.

1. *Lack of Organizational Readiness* Political conflict and upheavals similar to the situation mentioned above may minimize the opportunity for consultants to work effectively. In other cases, an organization may be undergoing radical internal change—reorganization, downsizing, or a merger. In such an environment, additional interventions by a consultant—for example, implementing a new performance management system—could be ineffective and even counterproductive. In both situations, there is a lack of organizational readiness that should alert the consultant to withdraw, sometimes only temporarily, until the timing is more favorable.

2. *Lack of Fit between Consultant Capability and Client Needs* As mentioned earlier, there are many types of management consultants and consulting firms. In some cases clients need specialized consulting services that a particular consultant or consulting firm cannot provide. For instance, a client may need consulting with regard to the technical, logistical aspects of a business merger, but mistakenly seeks out a consulting firm specializing in human resource development. If needs and capabilities are clarified early on, mismatches of this sort will become apparent, saving time and energy of both the consultant and the client.

3. *Inability to Accept Client's Goals or Policies* Remember that the client's goal is to run a successful business. But there are many different ways to do this. To be effective, consultants must be able to accept the client's goals as well as the means used to achieve those goals. If a consultant feels basically at odds with the client's business or management policies, the ethical response is to decline the assignment. One consultant, whose close relative developed lung cancer after many years of chain smoking, felt very uncomfortable working for the tobacco industry. After much soul searching, the consultant made a conscious decision to turn down assignments from that industry.

4. *Lack of Client Commitment* In some situations, clients may be ambivalent about a project and unwilling to cooperate with the consultant. For instance, in one project, a consulting firm was hired to conduct an organizational needs assessment. Typically, such a project includes a one- or two-day work conference with senior managers. At the work conference consultants present their findings and recommendations. They also work with senior managers to help them "own" the data and reach consensus over its implications. In this particular project, the company president refused to agree to a work conference. Instead, he insisted on a private four-hour feedback session with the consultants.

The assessment went very smoothly until the scheduled feedback session when the president arrived two hours late and left an hour early. Consistent with his lack of commitment, nothing was done with the results or the consultants' recommendations. Following this experience, the consulting firm established an unwritten rule not to sign a contract for an assessment unless key senior managers agreed to a work conference to process the findings and develop action plans.

As this case illustrates, when key players in an organization lack commitment to a project that requires their active support, the project is likely to fail. By accepting such a project, consultants help create expectations on the part of other organizational members—for example, the people interviewed—that will not be met. This often results in employee cynicism and even anger that is hard to dispell. Hence, if necessary commitment is lacking, consultants can best serve the prospective client organization by explaining their position and walking away.

The Client-Consultant Relationship

The previous example depicts a situation where the lack of client commitment compromised the outcome of a consulting project. But even when clients are fully committed, success cannot be taken for granted. One important determinant of a successful consulting project is the kind of relationship that consultants are able to forge with their clients and other key organizational members. This relationship involves mutual roles, expectations, and responsibilities.

Early in a consulting project, consultants must ask "who is the client?" This is often important because in most cases the client is *both* the business or organization as a whole *and* the individual who is the primary contact. Consultants need to be prepared for potential conflicts between the interests of the business organization represented by senior management and the individual contact. In the previous example, the consultant's primary organizational contact was not the senior managers but another member of the business. Nevertheless, senior management is still the client because if they do not buy into a project, it can die. Understanding the many roles and responsibilities of a client is an important part of the consultant's job. The role that the consultant chooses to adopt in the client relationship is important in managing the multiple client interests.

Common roles that consultants play include the expert role, the "pair of hands" role, and the collaborative or process consulting role (Block 1981). In the "expert" role, the consultant enters into a relationship with the client that is not unlike the doctor-patient relationship (Schein 1969). That is, the consultant is expected to possess all the knowledge and expertise necessary to diagnose organizational problems and come up with viable solutions. The client, on the other hand, remains relatively passive and dependent on the consultant for the answers. Of course, business clients are much less vulnerable than patients and may reject the consultant's advice at the end of the assignment. This is more likely to occur when little effort has been made to solicit client input and support during the course of the project.

To illustrate, an anthropologist was hired as a consultant by the State Department of Forests and Parks for a short-term summer project. The project was to develop a plan for a museum and walking tour at the site of a 16th-century sawmill. In effect, the anthropologist was hired as an expert consultant to the Department's Office of Information Services. The consultant spent three months in libraries, on sites, and meeting with individuals to gather appropriate data about the particular site. A 60-page report, which was written and submitted to the Office of Information Services, included maps for a museum plan and a walking tour, as well as the history and chronology of the site. These data were to be used in a public information brochure. As far as is presently known, the report was accepted, filed away and never acted upon.

This is a case in which the consultant acted as the "expert" by doing the research and providing a report that had the "answers" to the concerns. During the course of the project, the consultant worked very independently as an academic. Neither the Department of Forests and Parks nor the more direct project supervisor, the Director of the Office of Information Services, was involved during the data collection, planning or report writing. Of course, there are no guarantees that follow-up will necessarily occur after a research and planning effort. But it is more likely to occur if the consultant involves the clients so that they feel a personal commitment to the project and to seeing its recommendations implemented.

The second consultant role type is what Block calls the "pair of hands role." Here the consultant is relatively passive while the manager makes all the decisions. Often in the "pair of hands" role the consultant's goal is to improve the organization by adding technical expertise. The manager specifies what he or she wants, and the consultant produces while the manager evaluates on an ongoing basis.

The "pair of hands" role is typical of the relationship between a client and a software or information systems consultant. If the client is installing a new word processing system, the consultant will be hired to assist in setting up the equipment, training personnel and testing to see that there are no bugs. Key decisions about the system specifications have already been made and the consultant is hired primarily to implement those decisions. Continuous communication between the consultant and client is necessary because there are questions along the way that only the client can answer. At the same time, the client must be kept informed of the modifications to be sure that the changes meet the need.

The "pair of hands" role may be very appropriate to consulting assignments that focus on technological change. But in other contexts, the controlling client can make serious mistakes that could have been avoided through a more collaborative role with the consultant. For example, in one consulting case, the client—a middle manager who hired the consultant—insisted on revising the consultant's recommendations and presenting them to his superior, a senior manager. Initially the consultant objected, but then deferred to the client who had, from the beginning, wanted complete control over the project. The revised recommendations omitted some key points that the consultant had included based on his interviews with organization members. Unfortunately, the senior manager, who had expected information on those points, perceived the report as weak and summarily dismissed it. In this situation, the client could have benefited from following the consultant's advice rather than assuming that he, as the insider, knew what was best.

In contrast to both expert consulting and "pair of hands" consulting is the collaborative role, or what Schein refers to as process consulting: "a set of activities on the part of the consultant which help the client to perceive, understand, and act upon process events that occur in the client's environment" (1969:8–9). These process events can take place at the individual, interpersonal, and intergroup levels. With process consulting, consultants enter into a more collaborative relationship with clients who, in some cases, are actively involved in diagnosing and resolving organizational problems. Here, the consultant's role is not only to solve problems but to broaden management's competence in this and in similar areas.

To illustrate, in one situation the consultant was hired by the head of a small manufacturing company to diagnose and help resolve productivity and morale problems among workers. Through structured interviews the consultant learned that many employees perceived senior management as aloof and uninterested in the real problems workers faced "on the shop floor." Employees also felt that senior management was not leveling with them about the financial state of the company and what the future was likely to hold. The consultant not only conveyed the results of the interviews to senior management but worked with them to help them understand how their behavior could have shaped these perceptions. He also served as a coach, advising them on concrete ways to improve their management style. This included more "managing by wandering around" as well as periodic small group meetings with employees, where information was shared and questions were answered openly and honestly.

While expert and "pair of hands" consulting may be appropriate for certain situations, process consulting has important advantages. First, consultants work closely with members of the organization who can provide valuable data about its background, culture, and personalities. This kind of in-depth information, often necessary for valid analysis, would be difficult for consultants to come by independently in a relatively short time period. Second, by involving clients in the process, consultants gain their support for any ensuing recommendations, increasing the likelihood that these recommendations will be implemented once the consultant leaves the organization. Third, process consulting augments the client's understanding of his or her organization and minimizes dependence on the consultant. For example, in the previous case, once senior managers understood some of the causes of low productivity and morale, they were able to coach lower level managers to be more participative without relying on the external consultant.

Regardless of what role the consultant assumes, it is important that consultant and client try to clarify their responsibilities and expectations at the beginning of the project. And, since situations often change, it is equally important to reevaluate those expectations at key points throughout the project. All too often, unclear roles result in misunderstanding and damage to the consultant-client relationship. One typical misunderstanding arises when the client looks to the consultant as the expert, while the consultant adopts a more collaborative role, believing that client involvement is the key to successful organizational change. For instance, in a feedback session following an organizational needs assessment, comments from the consultant like, "Well, what do you think the implications are of what we uncovered during the interviews?" may confuse and even anger clients who expect a clear diagnosis and prescriptive solutions to organizational problems.

On the other hand, when the consultant assumes the expert role with clients who want to be more actively involved in the process, the consultant's prescriptive solutions will be rejected outright or, at best, tabled indefinitely. In either case, the consultant is misreading the clients' expectations and, as a result, assuming an ineffective role at a critical point in the project.

Wrapping up the Assignment

Regardless of what the contract states, the requirements of a consulting assignment often change throughout the course of the project. Things seem to continually evolve, requiring unanticipated time and effort. There is always more to be done, and, in some cases, consultants may have to renegotiate the contract to cover additional work necessary to the project's success. In any case, consultants should have an agreed-upon measure or date of completion with the client. Otherwise it is easy to become involved in continual discussions and meetings trying to wrap things up. This can be costly to a consultant in terms of time and money, which might be better used developing new business or working on another project. It can also lead to an unnecessary dependence on the consultant that gets in the way of clients' owning and managing the intervention that the consultant has helped initiate.

The Contributions of Anthropology

We have looked at some of the issues and challenges facing businesses today and examined management consulting—a profession dedicated to helping managers solve their business problems. In this chapter we focus on anthropology and the specific ways in which anthropological concepts and techniques can be incorporated into management consulting. For those readers who are unfamiliar with anthropology, we begin by answering the question, "What is an anthropological perspective?" We then turn to case examples that illustrate the application of this perspective. In each case, an anthropologist-management consultant used anthropological concepts and techniques to diagnose business problems and develop realistic recommendations for their solution.

What Is an Anthropological Perspective?

An anthropological perspective encompasses both a way of viewing the world and techniques for understanding that world. The key concept in anthropology is culture—loosely defined as the complex of beliefs, values, and related behavior shared by the members of a social group. For anthropologists, these cultural components are neither random nor haphazard. Rather, they form an internally logical and consistent adaptive system that helps people function successfully within their environment—physical and social. In other words, cultural beliefs and behavior have pragmatic value: they are intimately bound up with people's experiences in the real world. Correspondingly, cultural constructs make sense to the people who share them, even if their logic escapes outsiders.

The creation and sharing of cultural beliefs and values is an integral part of being human. Indeed, it is culture that makes social life possible. Therefore, the culture concept is as relevant to understanding the beliefs and behavior of social groups within a complex organization as it is to studying people in far away places.

Just as culture is found among all human groups, so is ethnocentrism—the implicit assumption that our own way of doing things (that is, our culture) is the best way or even the only way. Ethnocentric attitudes are common in complex organizations where different groups—for example, production and marketing, management and labor, home office and field operations—have difficulty acknowledging each other's problems, needs, and expectations.

Ethnocentrism is a real barrier to understanding people from other cultural (or subcultural) groups and to communicating effectively with them. Probably the best way to become aware of one's own implicit cultural patterns and overcome an ethnocentric attitude is to become a participant in another culture for an extended period of time.[7] Not surprisingly, the primary technique anthropologists use to study other cultures—*participant-observation*—involves living among a group of people, observing and recording their behavior, and participating in their daily lives as much as possible. The resulting account of a cultural system and its members is termed an *ethnography.*

While doing participant-observation, anthropologists try to adopt an *emic* approach, that is, uncovering "native" interpretations and meanings for events and behavior (Gamst 1977:3). These "native" images are recorded separately from the researcher's images—observations and interpretations. Thus, through a kind of "stereovision" (image of the left eye and image of the right eye) two distinct texts are created. These texts must be analyzed separately and then combined to reveal any differences. To resolve existing discrepancies, "native" informants should be asked to comment on the researcher's descriptions and explanation. These comments serve as a check on the researcher's ethnocentrism while adding greater depth to the "native" view (Werner and Schoepfle 1987:311). In the same way, discrepancies within the "native" text need to be uncovered and explained. Indeed, the richest accounts of a cultural system incorporate both contradiction and controversy as well as consensus (1987:312).

When anthropologists record and analyze cultural events and behavior, they view them *holistically,* as part of larger, integrated systems—economic, political, kinship, magico-religious. Holism is a valuable perspective that helps researchers avoid overly simplistic and reductionist explanations. Using a holistic analytical approach, anthropologists have uncovered important links between local, regional, national, and even international institutions—for example, businesses that transcend national boundaries (Wolfe 1977).

Anthropologists use a variety of data-gathering techniques in the field. Traditionally, these have been largely qualitative, and include structured and unstructured interviews; hypothetical situations; the analysis of critical events, social networks, myth and folklore, life histories; and historical reconstruction. Today, many anthropologists employ qualitative techniques along with more quantitative approaches (surveys, for example), especially if they are doing research in complex organizations (Pelto and Pelto 1978).

Even when quantitative and qualitative techniques are combined, some anthropologists argue that in-depth participant-observation (lasting at least several months) is the mainstay of valid anthropological research. During this extended time period, researchers can move through the ideal patterns (the "shoulds" and the "oughts"), to the believed patterns shared by informants, to modal behavioral patterns that researchers observe and participate in. Anything less does not qualify as a bona fide ethnography (Gamst 1980).

While fully supporting the merits of extended participant-observation, our own experience convinces us that many aspects of an anthropological perspective *can* be successfully employed by management consultants within a shorter time frame. The results will not be an ethnography (nor are they designed to be) but they can be complete enough to help consultants move beyond ideal patterns to understand the driving forces that shape belief and behavior in client organizations. These are the same forces that consultants must take into account when they help clients solve problems and implement organizational change.

In a recent monograph, Edgar Schein (1987) compares and contrasts the ethnographic method with the "clinical perspective" in process consulting. While Schein's discussion is useful, he misses some important parallels between the two approaches. For example, he states that, unlike ethnographers, consultants are brought into a situation by clients who want their help. Thus, the "gaining entry" problem that ethnographers have is not really an issue for consultants. Based on our experience, we would disagree with Schein. As we have pointed out, consultants are hired for a variety of reasons and not always by the people whose support and cooperation they need. Consultants are often brought into an organization by relatively powerless middle managers—frequently staff rather than line. Here, to effect any real change, the "power holders"—formal and informal—must be included in the process. This is a formidable challenge, not unlike gaining the support and confidence of informants in a field situation.

Schein also overlooks the key conceptual and methodological contributions that anthropology can make to consulting—for example, the use of an emic approach and the metaphor of "stereovision" to check ethnocentrism, ask relevant questions, and arrive at valid interpretations. And he neglects to mention how a holistic framework can counter an overly psychological "clinical" approach where consultants focus on the individual as the unit of analysis to the exclusion of larger social groupings.

Along with the conceptual and methodological contributions anthropology offers, there are specific analytical and research techniques from which management consultants can benefit. Indeed, the cases we present below demonstrate how these techniques have helped consultants deal with a wide range of business issues. In each case, consultants successfully used one or several of the following data-gathering and analysis tools.

1. *Structured Observations* Structured observations can be used in many organizational settings (on the shop floor, in the cafeteria, in the boardroom) to record lived beliefs and values as well as social relations. Although this technique provides rich data, it can be very time consuming.

Correspondingly, its use by management consultants may be limited by time and money constraints. (See Pelto and Pelto 1978:103–112 for discussion of types of data to be gathered from structured observations.)

2. *Interviews* Open-ended interviews are techniques that uncover people's ideas about selected aspects of organizational life—for example, rewards and recognition, labor-management issues, work-related problems and opportunities, subcultural beliefs and values. Interviews can be conducted with individuals as well as with groups. There are advantages and disadvantages to each approach. But, with each, the quality of the data collected depends largely on the interviewing skills of the consultant (as well as facilitation skills for group interviews). In any case, it is important to remember that what is being elicited is *stated perceptions* of organizational reality rather than that reality itself (Briggs 1986).

3. *Hypothetical Situations* Hypothetical situations can be created by asking informants a series of questions such as: "What would happen if. . . ? What would you typically do? Why would you make those choices? How would your boss respond?" Posing hypothetical situations in the context of an interview and probing for typical reactions get closer to organizational "reality" than standard questions because they encourage informants to talk about normative behavior patterns they have probably experienced (Werner and Schoepfle 1987:213–215).

4. *Critical Event Analysis* Similar to hypothetical situations, critical event analysis attempts to get at informants' "lived experiences" through the interview process.[8] Informants are asked to recall an event or a situation that they felt was critical to their success or failure on the job. The selection of the event and the detail in which it is recounted contain valuable information about how the informant perceives the world. Of course, observing the behaviors surrounding a critical event would be ideal. But consultants do not often have the opportunity to do this. Therefore, asking informants to recall a critical event and questioning them to recreate the behaviors, beliefs, and attitudes surrounding this critical event is the next best way to get at normative patterns and possible causes (if the critical event is problematic in nature).

5. *Network Analysis* Network analysis involves tracing the connections between individuals and groups, that is, who spends time with whom, when, where, and why. Data about these social links can be gathered through observations and/or interviews. Such data can be used to illuminate an organization's "informal" system including subcultural groups (Pelto and Pelto 1978:212–214).

6. *Content Analysis* Organizational documents, reports, speeches, and discussions at meetings provide a rich source of information that can be tapped through content analysis—examining the written and verbal data for common themes and patterns among the themes.

When the opportunity arises, these data can be compared with actual behavior to check for consistency as well as contradictions (see Pelto and Pelto 1978:113–115; Werner and Schoepfle 1987:208–239).

Unfortunately, there is no "cook book" formula to help consultants decide which technique to use in a particular situation. In our case examples, several factors affected the choice of a particular technique or set of techniques: (1) the information needed to understand the issue or problem and make valid recommendations; (2) the time and resources (including people and money) available; (3) the client's expectations. Often consultants must complement qualitative data with "numbers" to gain credibility among business managers; (4) consensus with other team members. Colleagues not trained in anthropology may have their own preferred techniques, so some internal negotiating may be necessary before a plan is presented to the client. (Of course, this is not a problem if the consultant is independent.)

Confidentiality of the Case Material

The issue of confidentiality is very important in the field of consulting and has ethical implications similar to those anthropologists confront with respect to their fieldwork. In the process of investigating an organization, consultants become privy to much information that is not available to others. It may be information that could damage the business if competitors had access to it. For example, consultants may understand production processes and techniques that give a company a cost advantage over competitors. The consulting process also frequently produces information that is potentially damaging to individuals within the company. In interviewing managers, consultants often get to know a particular individual's history. There may be some details that he or she does not wish to be public knowledge. The consultant has an ethical obligation to protect the rights of these individuals while working for the benefit of the total organization (the client). In light of the sensitivity of clients to the issue of confidentiality, many consulting firms have made it a practice not to disclose their client lists to the public.

The case examples in the following pages are all based on actual experiences. However, to protect our clients' interests and concern for confidentiality, we cannot provide the names and places of companies or people. Nor are we at liberty to present other details—however rich the data might be—that could inadvertently betray client confidentiality.

Cases: Managing Diversity

In the United States today there is much cultural diversity; for example, ethnic, gender, class, age, geographic region, as well as occupational or job-related differences are all associated with distinctive cultural attributes. Acknowledging the existence of these differences and their potential influence on employees is an important first step. But anthropologist-management consultants can go beyond this to understand such diversity by seeing the work environment emically—as employees perceive it. They can also employ appropriate information-gathering techniques such as those presented above to probe more deeply into cultural differences and understand how to best manage them.

Case 1 In this case, the consultant was hired to develop a training program for a client company that had recently created a new division combining employees from two functional groups, sales/marketing and technology. Although the division was only a few months old, communication and cooperation problems had already developed between the two groups. Sales/marketing complained that technology was not focused on customers' current needs, while technology felt that sales/marketing did not give them the data needed for their projects. During the two days the consultant visited the work site, she and a colleague interviewed members of both groups, probing their perceptions of what the problems were. Since the interviews were held on site, she could also observe interactions and talk informally with employees.

Through these techniques, the consultant discovered that the two groups differed along several lines other than their functional affiliation. Many of the technology employees were Asians who had some difficulty speaking English. They were, by and large, younger and more highly educated than their sales/marketing counterparts. Also, the technology employees were new hires while most employees in sales/marketing had been with the company for many years. All of these differences contributed to the communication and cooperation problems that were plaguing the new department. For example, one sales/marketing employee commented, "How can you work with these people. Some of them don't even speak English?" For their part, technology employees confided that they questioned the competence of some sales/marketing people who came up through the ranks and lacked higher education credentials.

These key findings were presented to the client (who had been largely unaware of their importance). They were also used in designing the training program intended to help each group see the other's perspectives. For example, the program included fictive case studies that captured some of the real misperceptions and behaviors of both groups. As they discussed the cases, participants were able to identify with events and characters (in a non-threatening way) and talk about how similar problems in their own work situation could be resolved. In another exercise each group was asked to clarify its own priorities and describe the priorities of the other group. Then the profiles—both self and other—were compared. Corresponding discussions centered around issues such as the following: how functional or disfunctional are our different priorities? How are misperceptions between us created? What can we do to better communicate our priorities and understand each other's needs? This kind of dialogue paved the way for more effective working relations between the two divisions once participants were back on the job.

Case 2 In this case, the consultant was hired by the medical directors of a large city hospital to evaluate a family medicine program that had been operating for about a year. The hospital's catchment area included individuals and families from diverse ethnic groups, many of whom were living at the poverty level. One of the program's objectives was to provide patients with timely access to family practitioners so they could avoid using emergency room services inappropriately. When the consultant entered the scene, program planners and health care providers shared their concern over the fact that many patients were reverting back to the emergency room as a source of first contact health care.

The consultant interviewed both patients and providers, using the hypothetical situation and critical events analysis techniques. As noted earlier, both get at informants' "lived experiences" and are the next best thing to actually observing them. Network analysis was also employed to investigate the health care behavior patterns of patients—for example, which family members and friends were involved in health care decisions. In addition, the consultant spent a good deal of time in the clinic setting, observing and talking informally to staff and patients. Many patients told interviewers that they had tried to use the telephone number their doctor or nurse had given them, but that no one answered. Some also complained about the disrespectful way they were treated by clerks in the clinic. As a result of both problems, they resorted to the emergency room.

The consultant's observations revealed that, indeed, telephones were often not answered, even when a clerk was next to the phone and unoccupied. When a clerk did respond, messages frequently were not delivered. And patients were sometimes treated very rudely by the clerks, either on the telephone or in person. Through informal conversations with clerks (and overhearing their comments to each other) the consultant learned that many of them—minority group members—felt looked down upon and even exploited by the hospital's medical and administrative staff. The clerks were very angry and this affected the way they treated patients.

When the consultant presented her report, clients were, at first, shocked and dismayed. But after accepting the finding, they began to make a real effort to improve relations with minority clerical employees. For example, they initiated conversations with these employees and created more flexible work schedules to meet their needs (several of the clerical employees were single mothers). At the same time, they engaged a special family practice clerk to take messages, relay information, and schedule appointments. They also established an answering service or "hot line" that bypassed the regular answering system so that patients could contact a family practitioner 24 hours a day. These changes not only solved the communication problems between patients and providers in the clinic but they also improved the working environment for professional staff, support staff, and patients alike.

Cases: Managing Complexity

Through a holistic and systems approach consultants and managers can view the organization as a complex and multidimensional organization—departments and divisions, corporate headquarters versus the field, hierarchical levels, international divisions and subsidiaries, and joint ventures. This goes far beyond the important but limited distinction between "formal" and"informal" systems with which many consultants and managers are familiar. A systems approach emphasizes the mutual dependence of all parts of the whole. Change in a part of the system will have implications for the whole operation. A holistic and systems approach to understanding organizational complexity can be of great value in planning and implementing necessary changes in today's volatile business world.

Case 3 In this situation, the consultant was hired by a company that had recently begun performance management training for all its managers. Performance management training is designed to give managers the concepts and skills they need to monitor, evaluate, and help improve the work performance of their employees. The consultant's mission was to revise the existing training program so that it would meet the specific needs of one functional group—sales—in the company. Many sales managers complained "The people at corporate headquarters don't really know our world: what it's like out in the field, and what we have to do to be successful. What's relevant when they evaluate their people may not be appropriate to us and our situation."

The consultant spent many hours working with one client, a sales manager who served as a key informant. Sales managers from several geographic districts were brought together for a group interview that included the use of hypothetical situations and critical event analysis. Through these techniques, the consultant was able to create a performance management training program that incorporated the issues and terminology of sales. At the same time, he was able to maintain the integrity of the formal, company-wide performance management training program while substituting sales-specific alternatives where appropriate. For example, the company-wide program emphasized the importance of "managing by wandering around"—informally visiting employees at their work sites—impossible for sales managers since their employees were scattered over a wide geographic territory. In the revised program, the value of staying in touch with employees was emphasized but other methods for accomplishing this, such as informal telephone conversations, were introduced. The sales force accepted these changes and bought into the company's overall performance management system.

Case 4 Here, the consulting situation involved working with senior managers in a large company to help them implement a quality improvement process. As a first step, the consulting team conducted a company-wide needs assessment. At the urging of the anthropologist-consultant, the clients agreed to include employees at all levels of the company in the assessment. Formerly, only higher-level employees had participated in company-sponsored research.

During the needs assessment, consultants conducted unstructured interviews at various work locations and administered a survey to all employees. Interview and survey data plus observations at work sites soon revealed a major *cultural* split between managers and non-managerial employees. Additional data supporting this finding came from the consultants' participation and observations at executive meetings. For example, at first, senior managers told consultants that "everyone in the company had participated in a recent employee survey." They repeated this several times until asked if "everyone" included hourly and clerical workers. At that point senior managers acknowledged that these lower level employees had not participated in the survey. Confirming these observations some lower level employees told consultants, "We are invisible around here. Management doesn't even know we exist." The split between management and nonmanagement ranks resulted in low morale and distrust of management on the part of many workers. In such an environment, quality improvement efforts had little chance of success.

In this case, consultants combined anthropological techniques—content analysis, hypothetical situation and critical event analysis—with some key consulting skills—facilitation and consensus building—to both analyze the data and present the findings in a culturally appropriate way to senior managers. As a result, senior managers overcame their initial shock and resistance and accepted the consultants' findings and recommendations. To reduce the gap between managers and nonmanagers and involve all employees in quality improvement they began training every employee in quality awareness and supporting team-based problem solving for employees at all levels. In the latter case, teams not only empowered employees but they significantly reduced costly quality problems such as waste and rework.

Case 5 In this situation, a consultant was hired by a small suburban town to design and run a management training program for the town directors and department heads. The town had received a grant from the state to provide training in goal setting, time management, team building, delegation, and communication for the directors and department heads. This group included the Chief of Police, Fire Chief, Youth Services Director, Recreation Director, Public Health Commissioner, Sewer Commissioner, Town Clerk, Executive Secretary and his Assistant, the Town Accountant, the Assistant Tax Collector, etc. In short, all individuals who were responsible to elected officials and served in a managerial capacity for the town (except for those in the School Department) were to be part of the training program.

The town published a request for proposals for the training. The consultant who was hired suggested that the training be designed to meet the particular needs of the town. The training would encompass the targeted skills such as goal setting and time management but would not necessarily be divided according to these arbitrary categories. Rather, the framework for the program would reflect the overall town issues and specific management skills would be addressed within this framework. In order to determine these issues, the consultant proposed that all designated participants of the training be interviewed individually.

In the data gathering and analysis stage open-ended interviews included some standardized questions about the particular skills identified in the grant. During the course of the interviews, which took place over a period of six weeks, the consultant was able to establish a relationship with the managers who would be participating in the training program.

The data analysis revealed that the organization had little sense of shared values. There was little trust or cooperation across departments. Self-protection and justification for actions emerged as common patterns.

The design of the training program had to address these issues, meet the Executive Director's needs and also meet the stated objectives in the request. The greatest challenge in designing the training program was to provide something that would help establish a sense of mission, develop an awareness and sense of the importance of working *together* instead of against each other, while at the same time meeting the more specific requirements of developing managerial skills such as goal setting.

The consultant's anthropological perspective helped clients understand the "big picture" that influenced their behavior and that of their colleagues. The town administration was a system responding to voters, elected officials, state officials and federal regulations. When participants learned to see the town government in this context, many of the attitudes and behaviors exhibited by other officials began to make sense. For example, the Town Accountant had complained that the Tax Collector's office was slow and uncooperative in posting the collected taxes. But he found out that the Tax Collector believed he was following the law, which said that citizens who had filed a request for adjustment were to be granted a period of time to have the request heard before they had to pay.

Case 6 This consulting situation involved a manufacturing company that was losing significant market share in an increasingly competitive environment. As part of the organizational needs assessment, the consultant interviewed managers and employees at all levels in the company around their perceptions of what customers wanted. She also interviewed several of the client company's key customers—related manufacturers whose base of operations was in a different part of the country. By gathering stories as well as critical incidents from customers, the consultant was able to piece together the customers' perspective and present that to the client company. This perspective included the feeling that customer and client company "lived in two different worlds." Indeed, regional cultural differences as well as different economic pressures contributed to communication problems between the client company and its customers. Acting as a kind of "culture broker" (Chambers 1985:26) the consultant conveyed this message with concrete examples of how customer needs and requirements had not been understood. For example, customers complained that late delivery of merchandise crippled their operations and made it impossible to meet *their* customers' demands. And when their customers weren't satisfied, they could very easily go elsewhere. Corresponding recommendations helped the client company bridge the very real gaps between themselves and their customers. The new action clients took included on-site visits to the customers' work environment, to experience their needs and pressures first-hand.

Cases: Interpreter of Processes and Events

In an earlier chapter, we talked about process consulting wherein consultants collaborate with their clients to help them better understand and thus manage their own organizational patterns. An anthropological perspective can be particularly valuable in process consulting—even to the point of helping colleagues understand their own professional culture. The following cases illustrate this, focusing on the consultant's role as interpreter of organizational events and processes.

Case 7 This case describes a situation in which the consultant was part of a team called in to help a nonprofit organization improve the performance of middle and lower level managers. Senior management felt that the organization was not working efficiently and that there were some motivational and morale problems among the managers. They wanted to create a performance management system to improve the effectiveness of these managers.

As part of the project, the consulting team interviewed middle managers. The interview questions were designed to learn which behaviors were effective and helpful to the organization and which were not. While the senior management of the organization focused on individual managers, the consultants looked for broader cultural patterns that managers shared. They also attempted to understand what motivated the middle managers to act in specific ways, even if those patterns were not benefiting the organization.

The interviews revealed that the organization was driven by a "culture of volunteerism" at work on all levels. Therefore, being nice and getting along with everyone was highly valued and influenced many behaviors. This often appeared inefficient to senior management because it interfered with accomplishing more measurable tasks. The "culture of volunteerism" was deeply rooted in the organization because many volunteers were used in field situations and many managers had been hired into their positions after years of serving as volunteers. Their reason for working was not to set measurable goals and get results. Rather, working meant that one was a good person because one was engaged in performing a service to society.

Consultants were able to interpret events and processes in this organization that contributed to this "culture of volunteerism." Based on these findings, the action they recommended went beyond performance management training for individuals to looking for ways either to *use* the "culture of volunteerism" to further organization objectives, or to *change* this cultural pattern so that it no longer constituted a barrier to managerial effectiveness.

Case 8 In this situation, one of the authors gave a "brown bag" luncheon presentation in her consulting firm, focusing on the company's "rites of passage" for new consultants. As a participant-observer in that setting, she was able to understand how new consultants were initiated into the fast track. She demonstrated her findings through role playing, a widely accepted training technique in this and other consulting firms. The role play, which portrayed a typical day in the life of a new consultant, was both humorous and insightful.

By facilitating a discussion of the role play (rather than lecturing), the consultant was able to help colleagues understand aspects of their organizational culture that were reflected and reinforced through informal rites of passage. For example, it was common to send a new consultant with little experience out on a field assignment. In this situation, novice consultants often felt they had been thrown into the water to "sink or swim." Although sometimes painful, this rite of passage served an important purpose. It highlighted the value that the company placed on consultants who were "quick studies," self-starters, and tolerant of ambiguity and change. It also revealed—perhaps for the first time in a public forum—the pain that new consultants experienced. Over time, the company made some important changes, for example, a formal orientation program, to minimize that pain and better prepare new consultants for their assignments.

A Caveat: The Misuse of the Culture Concept

In 1970, Margaret Mead commented on the misuse of the culture concept. "Today there is almost no resemblance between the concept of culture based on the work of the field anthropologist . . . and the concept based on his work that is used in contemporary scientific thought. From the standpoint of what the psychologist, sociologist or historian attempts to understand, the model of . . . culture has lent itself to a kind of extrapolation that is crude, deterministic and reductionist" (1970:xxiii).

Management consultants using an anthropological perspective should be aware that similar misuses of the culture construct exist in the contemporary business world. When consultants discuss the importance of "culture" colleagues and clients may have very different images of what organizational culture is all about. For example, the term "corporate culture" is frequently cited to describe the general beliefs and values of an organization.[9] This popular usage can be grossly misleading when it overlooks organizational diversity and reduces workplace beliefs, values, and behavior to a homogeneous, monolithic entity created by senior management. As a result, senior management is led to believe that they can change their corporate culture overnight with a few speeches, training programs, or even radical interventions. To illustrate this fallacy and the serious problems it can generate, we present the now classic case of Bill Agee, a senior manager who undertook to change the culture and business of the Bendix Corporation. The Agee story is a well-known one and was much publicized by the media as the events unfolded in the late 1970s. Because of this, we can describe relevant events and key players much more openly than with our own client cases where confidentiality must be respected.

Bill Agee, a Harvard Business School graduate and promising young executive at Boise Cascade, joined Bendix Corporation in 1972. He was made Chairman and CEO in 1976 when the former CEO, Michael Blumenthal, left to take a post as Secretary of the Treasury in the Carter administration. Agee had a strategic vision for a new corporate strategy for Bendix. He wanted to "transform a nondescript automotive and aerospace supplier into a glamorous, high-flying, high-technology company" (*Fortune,* 3 November 1980, p. 48). In order to accomplish this he would have to transform the organization, that is, change the "culture."

Bendix Corporation was a large, lumbering, corporate conglomerate with a number of businesses including Autoparts and Forest Products. When Agee took over, Bendix was performing poorly due to recessions in these two industries. Agee was determined to change Bendix. He wanted to reduce the company's dependence on the automotive industry and get into faster growth industries. In order to do that, he would sell off less profitable businesses, build a cash reserve and buy his way into the high technology club. He knew that in order to make the business changes really work, there would have to be some important changes in the company's "corporate culture."

A viable competitor in a high technology business must be able to adapt to changes in requirements very quickly. A company such as Bendix was not equipped to respond in these kind of ways. Agee tried to begin the process of cultural change with some highly visible symbolic changes. For example, he removed the conference table from the Board room, thus indicating to the staid and conservative Board that things were going to change and there was nowhere to hide. He freed up the executive parking lot and the executive cafeteria, indicating that the old executive pecking order was no longer viable. He held "mind stretch sessions" with personalities such as Vernon Johnson and Gloria Steinem to convey the message to prepare for a "new age."

Along with these symbolic changes Agee made some business changes. He reorganized. When the executive vice-president for strategic planning at Bendix resigned, Agee hired 29-year-old Mary Cunningham, right out of Harvard Business School. He made the company's French subsidiary profitable by trimming jobs and selling off parts of the company. He sold the Forest Products division. He bought and sold stock in other companies to build a nest egg, which he intended to use to buy his way into his vision of Bendix in the future. He targeted the Autoparts division in a study of strategic viability to the long-term future of Bendix.

Many of these moves were in direct violation of the "way things are done around here," but Agee pressed on assuming that he was addressing the "cultural" issues and that his vision of the "new Bendix" could become a reality.

It is unlikely that Agee's ill-conceived foray into culture change would have achieved the reeducation of Bendix's work force. His experiment was terminated when he lost a takeover shootout and was forced to resign.

Bill Agee recognized the need to change the organization "culture" in order to implement his strategy. He made some symbolic changes, such as removing the Board table, which he thought would facilitate the "new direction" he envisioned. However, he underestimated the considerable resistance to such radical change that occurred throughout the organization. People were used to having a hierarchy, a place to sit at the table, and a place to park their cars. These practices helped structure their work environment, define their roles, and give them meaning.

When Agee disrupted all this, he created uncertainty, fear, and distrust. It is difficult to muster an organization that distrusts its Chief. Had Agee looked for ways to harness the existing belief systems, hierarchy, and social networks to promote the changes he wanted, he might have been more successful. Instead he chose to take them apart. At the end of the day, Agee lost his company and his job by not fully comprehending the dimensions and the depth of a company culture, including the fact that deeply embedded cultural beliefs and practices will persist despite many directives from the top.

Management consultants using an anthropological perspective can help their colleagues and clients understand the subtleties and complexities of culture and thus avoid the kinds of simplistic assumptions made by Agee. At the very least, they will realize that it takes more than a plan for change and a few radical interventions to transform deeply embedded cultural beliefs, values, and behavior. More positively, they will be able to harness anthropological concepts and techniques to deal with concrete issues in ways that the case examples presented above illustrate.

Management Consulting Knowledge and Skills

In each of the cases presented earlier, the consultant combined an anthropological perspective with management consulting knowledge and skills. Here we look more closely at the knowledge and skill sets that consultants need to be effective. This section is addressed particularly to those practitioners in anthropology who wish to pursue a career in management consulting.

Context Knowledge and Skills

First of all, it is essential that management consultants understand the broader environment within which client companies operate. This includes macro-level business trends—industry dynamics, politics, economics, technology, demographics—on an international as well as a national level. They also need to know about the specific issues relevant to particular industries (financial, manufacturing, telecommunications, public utilities, governmental, health care). These issues include, but are not limited to, competition, market share, revenue, profits, and customer satisfaction. Consultants then have to be able to relate both these industry-specific issues and macro-level business trends to the problems and opportunities facing the client company. Indeed, a common question prospective clients pose is, "What do you know about *our* business?"

To communicate their knowledge and experience to clients, consultants should also be familiar and comfortable with business language and general cultural patterns—business terminology including finance and money, verbal and nonverbal behavior, and power relations. This kind of context understanding is important in all consulting situations, both to establish credibility and to work effectively.

Most business courses at colleges and universities can provide aspiring consultants with a framework for understanding the context of business operations. For example, a good "Introduction to Business" course will expose participants to business language and help them understand the functional areas of business. Careful reading of business press such as *Business Week, Fortune, Forbes* and the *Wall Street Journal* can offer more specific information about industry trends, markets and technologies.

Content skills are more specialized. Aspiring consultants must decide what their focus will be and then spend some time learning the content of that area. There is a large body of literature on nearly every area of management consulting, including performance management, organizational design and development. Graduate schools of education usually offer courses that include theories of adult learning. There are also specialized courses such as "Human Resource Management" or "Organizational Design" offered in graduate schools of business. Additionally, consulting firms and training and development divisions of companies will have developed their own libraries. Acquiring content skills means reading, listening, and watching. Creating opportunities to watch other consultants at work is one of the best ways to learn how content is integrated into the context of actual consulting work.

As the cases presented earlier exemplify, some consulting projects involve the creation of training and educational programs in areas such as performance management, quality improvement, and management development. To complete these projects successfully, consultants need program development skills—designing and writing educational material that corresponds with the principles of adult learning as well as with the client organization's culture and specific needs.

Along with the above, consultants should have strong analytical skills, quantitative as well as qualitative. Some common consulting situations where these skills apply include organizational and human resource needs assessments, strategic planning, process consulting, and marketing research. For example, the organizational needs assessments discussed in several of the cases described earlier involved both surveys and in-depth qualitative interviews. The challenge consultants face is to bring qualitative and quantitative data together to create a valid and useful picture of the client's organization. This challenge is heightened by the fact that consultants usually have a limited amount of time to investigate an organization. Hence, they must also possess the ability to do quick (but accurate) analyses and develop realistic recommendations.

Process Knowledge and Skills

In addition to context and content skills, management consultants need process skills to work effectively. These include facilitation, that is, the ability to manage group discussions and group process so individuals learn and group members feel the experience is positive. It is important for prospective consultants with a strong academic background to understand that facilitation is very different from most kinds of teaching. Unlike the teacher, the facilitator is an *enabler* of group learning rather than the *expert*. Strong facilitation skills are necessary in many consulting situations, such as leading training and educational workshops, leading work conferences, and process consulting. As most consultants have witnessed, even the most carefully designed training workshop or conference can fall flat with poor facilitation. Conversely, a strong facilitator can make weak training material "sing" by being in touch with the group's needs and modifying the workshop accordingly.

To identify and meet the needs of their clients, management consultants should possess knowledge about individual and group behavior and strong interpersonal skills in managing conflict, building teams, and striving for consensus. These interpersonal skills are not emphasized in the academic institutions where anthropologists are trained, where heated theoretical debates, peer critiques (not always constructive), and "one-upmanship" prevail (Schein 1987). Nevertheless, they are necessary in most consulting situations, such as leading workshops and work conferences and process consulting. For example, in Case 4 presented above, the consultant used facilitation and interpersonal skills to help clients overcome their initial resistance to the assessment data, and to accept the findings and reach consensus over appropriate action. These same process skills also contribute to successful one-on-one collaboration between consultant and client and among consultants working on the same project.

Process skills are best acquired from practice and feedback. For this reason, consulting firms often have their own internal training process. They usually trust that their consultants can acquire context and content skills from reading, listening, and watching. But process skills require "doing" as well as understanding. Some firms run sessions for young consultants where participants can practice on each other.

Independent or aspiring consultants who do not have access to these resources must explore other opportunities to gain process skills. Professional organizations, including the American Anthropological Association, sometimes hold seminars and workshops for members interested in learning training skills and techniques. For example, at the 1984 Annual Meetings, an anthropologist doing cross-cultural training ran a training session for a day in advance of the meetings. Another organization to investigate is ASTD (The American Society for Training and Development). Some additional ways to practice process skills and get feedback include running academic seminars in a facilitative manner and volunteering to run meetings or lead group activities. Many consultants have found that, when possible, videotaping one's performance is a great way to see yourself as others see you. This allows you to target both your process strengths as well as areas that need improvement.

Becoming a Management Consultant

An anthropologist-management consultant is a bridge between two very different fields. The benefits of acting as the bridge are many; they include enriching both sides. The risks are also great because bridges tend to be targeted from both sides. The following experience is one type of reaction that an anthropologist-management consultant might get from some academic anthropologists.

The consultant had just finished facilitating a five-day training program for hospital managers. The program was designed to help managers motivate subordinates by using more participatory management styles in which employees would become more involved in the decision-making process. The consultant knocked on the office door of one of her former anthropology professors. He invited her in to chat. When she began to explain what she had been doing during the year since they last met, he responded "So . . . you sold out, huh?" Presumably the implication was that by working for "management" the anthropologist had betrayed the workers of the world.

The initial stages of transfer into the field of consulting are lonely. Many old academic friends wonder *why* you would want to get into business training. There is a widening gap between the mainstream anthropology from graduate school and what you are trying to do.

At the same time, it may be unwise to openly confess to a past life as an anthropologist, because one can never be sure what images that will conjure up for bosses, colleagues or clients. Anthropologists have a reputation among many business people of being a bit flaky and unpredictable. After all, who would really *want* to go and live among natives or dig up skeletons? For example, one anthropologist-consultant casually mentioned his background at an initial meeting with senior manager clients. The reaction was nervous laughter followed by comments such as, "Why are you here with us? We're not monkeys, are we?" and, "I don't know if I like the idea of being 'studied' by an anthropologist." Following that experience, the consultant kept his former life "in the closet" with clients until their working relationship had demonstrated that he was both competent and trustworthy.

Gaining Entry into the Field

How does one actually bridge the two fields of anthropology and management consulting? It is highly unlikely that an anthropologist with a straight academic resume would be considered for a consulting position, either by a firm or a prospective client. So how can one gain the necessary skills outlined earlier and the credentials to appear credible in the consulting and business world? One way is the formal route of taking business courses or even getting an MBA degree. Other, more adventurous approaches, include (1) becoming an "apprentice" to an independent consultant; (2) securing a temporary assignment or an internship with a consulting firm. The latter might involve writing a proposal for a particular project. Ideally, one should combine the approaches so that necessary formal knowledge and skills come alive through actual experience. Indeed, the challenges of becoming a management consultant are similar to the challenges of doing field research. While there are many books and articles written on the topic, the *experience* of doing it will be very different from abstract theorizing. And, as an earlier case illustrated, one's first few consulting assignments are important "rites of passage" into a new professional identity.

With one foot in the door, the anthropologist-consultant faces the real credibility test—success with clients. This is the most important criterion used by other consultants (and prospective clients) as they evaluate your contribution to their firm.

Developing a client relationship that is based on mutual trust and respect takes hard work. It is similar to gaining the respect of powerful informants in the field. Clients need to feel that you speak their language well, that you are honest and trustworthy, and that you have something to offer them that will help them meet their goals.

Along with mastering the knowledge and skills presented earlier, there are some general guidelines for successful consulting. These have much in common with guidelines for doing good fieldwork: (1) learn the client's language and business; (2) expect the unexpected; (3) keep an open mind; (4) monitor your influence on the organization; (5) act with honesty and integrity.

1. *Learn the Client's Language and Business* To complement their general business knowledge, consultants must prepare for each assignment by educating themselves as fully as possible about the client's language, norms, work processes, and business issues. As a case in point, one consultant just completed what he thought was a very successful initial meeting with a group of senior managers. When he asked for feedback, the managers said that his misuse of some key industry-specific terms made them think that he really didn't understand their business.

In accessing client-specific information, consultants should look for "key informants" in the company—employees who can provide them with necessary data or lead them to appropriate sources.

2. *Expect the Unexpected* As with field research, no matter how much you prepare for a consulting experience, it is bound to be different.

Successful consulting means being able to anticipate the unexpected and "turn on a dime" if necessary. For example, a consultant was preparing to meet with a group of senior managers for the first time to plan an organizational needs assessment. Days before the meeting, one key senior manager had been replaced by someone new. Anticipating how this might affect group dynamics, the consultant came to the meeting armed with a range of material that included background information, success stories from other clients, and team-building exercises. As it turned out, that supplementary material was invaluable, because the day was spent less on planning the assessment and more on integrating the new player into the process and getting his support.

3. *Keep an Open Mind* Effective consulting requires an ability to listen, to listen, and to listen. As with anthropological research, time and again there will be data that contradict other information. It is quite common to get conflicting diagnoses of an organization's problems from different individuals. For example, when consultants interviewed the president of an actuarial firm, his perception of the most pressing problem was that project teams did not integrate well with each other. For their part, team leaders felt that the greatest problem the organization and project teams faced was getting information from the president.

It is important for consultants to remain open to all sorts of data—indeed, to actively seek out information from different sources. As one seasoned consultant put it, "Understand the challenges that your main contacts are struggling with and touch base with them continually. However, don't assume that what they tell you is the whole truth. Look beyond them to their bosses, their employees, and other critical players and be prepared with advice that goes beyond just what they are asking for."

4. *Monitor Your Influence on the Organization* As anthropologists know from fieldwork, the very presence of an outsider in any capacity changes the nature of the social phenomena being observed. This is equally true for consultants. The process of consulting is an intervention that will have effects. If the intervention is conducted well, the effects will be positive, as in the case of a large inner-city hospital. Here, consultants and the client worked hard to prepare managers for a project that involved meetings with the consultants to discuss managerial successes and problems. As a result, managers willingly cooperated. They felt that the hospital was taking an interest in their jobs and their world. And the interviews themselves served as vehicles to open discussions around the "level of service" required by most hospital jobs.

On the other hand, interventions that are mishandled can create unnecessary damage, such as anxiety, resentment, or resistance from participants. This is the case when interviewees are not adequately prepared—for example, when they are not told the purpose of the interivew, why *they* were chosen, or what will be done with the data. It is incumbent on consultants to prevent these kinds of problems by laying the necessary groundwork before they begin an intervention and by monitoring their impact throughout the process.

5. *Act with Honesty and Integrity* For consultants, honesty and integrity include promising clients only what you can deliver and acting in their best interests at all times. It also means protecting the rights of clients and other organizational members. For example, consultants should guarantee confidentiality to employees who provide them with information. In one case, the Chief Executive Officer of a client company cornered the consultant and asked him what employee X had divulged in an interview. The consultant refused to answer, explaining that he had promised confidentiality to interviewees. He also emphasized the need to gain the trust and confidence of employees if the proposed intervention were to succeed. This was the appropriate response, even if it had jeopardized the consultant's position—which, fortunately, did not happen.

Life in the Fast Lane

Once consultants have established their credibility and are actively employed, what shape will their lives take? First of all, most independent and firm-based consultants travel a great deal, regionally, nationally, and even internationally. Indeed, some firms require that consultants spend at least 50% of their time on the road. Some consultants regard this as a real plus, while others, including those with families, have more difficulty adjusting. A typical work week in the life of a consultant might look like this:

Monday:	9–11 am—Meetings in-house 11 am–1 pm—Work on assessment report 2–3 pm—Conference call with client #1 3:00 pm—Leave for airport; fly to Dayton 7:00 pm—Have dinner with client #2 10–12 pm—Prepare for next day's workshop
Tuesday:	7:00 am—Set up equipment in conference room 8:00 am—Begin day 1 of a 3-day workshop 12:00 pm—Break for lunch; respond to voice mail 5:00 pm—End day 1 6:00 pm—Respond to voice mail 7:00 pm—Have dinner with participants 10–12 pm—Prepare for next day's workshop
Wednesday:	(similar to Tuesday)
Thursday:	(similar to Tuesday up to 5 pm) 6:00 pm—Leave for airport; fly to Newark 9:00 pm—Respond to voice mail 9:45 pm—Call colleague to discuss client #1-related problem and strategize 11–12 pm—Prepare for next day's interviews

Friday:

7:00 am—Have breakfast with client #1
7:45 am—Arrive at client's headquarters
8:00 am—Begin needs assessment interviewing process (three individual interviews from 8 am to 1 pm)
1:00 pm—Break for lunch; eat while answering voice mail
1:30 pm—Resume interviewing (1 individual and 1 group interview from 1:30 to 5 pm)
5:00 pm—Leave for airport; fly home (plane delayed 2 hours)
8:50 pm—Arrive home

As this sketch reveals, a consultant's days are long and filled with movement. There is current business, future business, and past business to manage each day. All of these involve communication with colleagues as well as clients. The day does not end at 5 pm when the client session is officially over. In fact, much important work is done informally—over dinner, for example. During dinner, consultants can find out how the day went for clients, whether or not their expectations were met, and what should be done differently tomorrow. These informal contacts not only provide valuable information, they help forge the personal trust and confidence so central to successful client relationships.

The consulting lifestyle is highly challenging and stimulating—working with many different types of clients in diverse settings. As a consultant, one can apply analytic skills to concrete issues and problems and enjoy the satisfaction of seeing results. In the words of one colleague, "When I record the ideas and suggestions of employees and convey them to the people (senior managers) who can make a difference, I feel good. When I see those differences, I feel great." The advantages of being a successful consultant also include financial rewards. Starting salaries in most management consulting firms are far above what an anthropologist might earn in academia. So, for a practicing anthropologist whose temperament is conducive to a quick-paced lifestyle with heavy demands as well as rewards, management consulting is worth exploring.

A Note to Managers

Clearly, managers have much to gain by hiring consultants with an anthropological perspective to help them with their business issues. But managers themselves will increasingly be called upon to extend their roles and, at times, even act as "internal consultants" in their own organizations.

Many organizations have their own training and organizational development departments. The purpose of these staff divisions is to act as internal consultants to line managers. Ideally, internal consultants are always on the spot so that they can anticipate issues as they arise and address them before they develop into real problems. But the role of an internal consultant is one that managers can also take on. By stepping into the role of internal consultant, managers are better prepared to diagnose problems as they occur, thus providing more flexible and timely response. As internal consultants, managers can use the same anthropological concepts and methods that external consultants employ.

For example, a department manager of a retail store may notice that during one shift the department runs smoothly, while it seems chaotic during another shift. In the first case, displays are neat and well stocked. Salespeople are prompt, friendly, courteous and organized. Sales receipts tend to be greater. On the other shift, the department seems unorganized. Racks get moved. Displays run out of stock. Salespeople are late, unavailable or too busy to help customers. Sales receipts are lower. In this situation, a good department manager will act as her own consultant and research the problem, analyze the causes, diagnose the situation, and decide what to do to improve the overall functioning of the department.

First, she must gather more data in order to understand the problem at hand. The data gathering might include some structured observations in each of two shifts when displays are set up and taken down. Interviews with shift supervisors and salespeople will provide data about how each perceives the situation. Network analysis can lead to some understanding of the kinds of relationships structuring the lives of supervisors and salespeople. For example, there might be a very important relationship between a salesperson and an accounting clerk on the 7th floor that tends to take the salesperson to the accounting department at the slightest excuse. Or, there could be a system problem—during the second shift the central computer was often down for repairs so that the cash registers were slow.

Some organizational experts predict that the most important role (middle) managers will have in the future is that of system integrator. This includes data gathering, information sharing, and mutual consultation among organizational units (Oshry 1982). When they assume the role of system integrator, managers will help break down the endemic barriers and "turfism" that exist among divisions, departments, and functional groups in many U.S. companies. To illustrate, marketing managers can convey important information to the manufacturing branch of an industry about customer preferences that will help manufacturing adjust their operations to meet customer needs. Correspondingly, manufacturing managers can consult with marketing about operations capabilities and realistic time frames to help marketing shape customer expectations.

To function as system integrators, managers will need to broaden their perspectives and, perhaps, learn some new skills. For all of the reasons discussed earlier, we suggest that anthropology be included in these new approaches.

Benefits from the Exchange

We have looked carefully at the benefits of an anthropological perspective for management consultants and their business clients. In this final section we examine what anthropology as a discipline can gain from the increased contact and collaboration with management consulting and the wider business world. The three broad areas of benefit that we focus on include practice, research, and teaching.

Practice

Over the past few years, the number of practicing anthropologists has been growing rapidly. For example, membership in the National Association of Practicing Anthropologists has risen significantly. As practitioners in a wide variety of settings, anthropologists often have the opportunity to use the consulting skills outlined above—even if their work is not labeled "consulting" per se. A knowledge of adult learning and the ability to facilitate group processes, build teamwork and consensus, and manage conflict are valuable and often essential tools in any organizational context. Moreover, when practicing anthropologists demonstrate a realistic grasp of how economic and environmental variables affect particular issues, they help establish their credibility among other pragmatically oriented professionals.

In an important sense, management consultants can serve as role models for anthropologists interested in practice. Consultants are trained to think practically in terms of tangible issues, actions, and results. Measures of success in a consulting project are not how many publications ensue but, rather, what is *done* with the findings and corresponding recommendations. Anthropologists can benefit from this "action" perspective since, in most cases, their formal training has emphasized theory to the exclusion of its practical applications.

As practicing anthropologists develop and exhibit competence in all of these areas, they will become more marketable outside of academia and thus create new job opportunities for people with anthropological training. Some of these new opportunities including working as management consultants and combining "the best of both worlds" to meet the needs of business clients.

Research

By collaborating with and working as management consultants, practicing anthropologists can help clarify and refine our understanding of many important topics: complex organizations, organizational change, decision making, diversity in the workplace, and the international division of labor. Theories that appear impressive in the classroom or in scholarly writings may prove very limited when applied to concrete research situations. Testing these theories in a variety of real-world settings will reveal their gaps as well as strengths and provide data for revision. There are numerous examples of this—Baba's research on the value of employee's "local knowledge systems" (1988a), and M. R. Louis's work taking the culture concept beyond content to include the roots "sourcing" as well as the extent "bounding" or shared understanding (1985).

During the course of research, anthropologists and management consultants can determine which methods and data-gathering techniques are most useful for quick but valid analyses of organizational and workplace reality. For example, in several of the cases cited above, consultants used hypothetical situations and critical event analysis to uncover key processes and relations within the client organization. They were able to accomplish this without engaging in lengthy participant-observation. At the same time, new methods and techniques appropriate for nontraditional settings can be developed. Some recent innovations by anthropologist-consultants include the development of "ethnohistorical mapping" to determine the feasibility of joint ventures (Baba 1988b), and the use of "semantic scanning" to reveal the tacit assumptions and definitions used by organizational members at all levels to see their environment.[10]

Most probably, these new methods and techniques will include a mix of qualitative and quantitative research approaches. On the one hand, an anthropological perspective can help prevent consultants from falling into the trap of statistical superficiality (Kirk and Miller 1986). But, at the same time, the questions and needs of business clients will force anthropologists to complement their more qualitative techniques with appropriate quantitative methods. One way to describe the mix is to use quantitative data—for example, organizational survey profiles—as the "bones" or "skeleton," while corresponding qualitative data provide the "meat" in the form of concrete examples, events, explanations, stories, and interpretation.

As practicing anthropologists increasingly enter the "corporate jungle" (Zemke 1989) and demonstrate the practical utility of an anthropological perspective, they enhance the potential for corporate funding of basic anthropological research. This will benefit individual researchers and the discipline of anthropology as well as the research sponsors.

Teaching

Teaching is an activity that occupies many anthropologists. Here is an opportunity to influence the next generation, to make a contribution to the values behavior of future citizens. But to have a real and lasting effect on students, teachers must provide relevant content material in engaging and thought-provoking ways. The collaboration between anthropology and management consulting can contribute to both these areas.

When we think about the tens of thousands of students who enroll in anthropology courses each year, we can ask ourselves, "What do they take with them at the end of the course?" Some are probably turned on to anthropology as a new and exciting field of study. Others may be nonplussed. And some are turned off, only thinking about the fact that they have managed to fulfill one more distribution requirement. In three to five years most of these students will become part of the work force and many of them will eventually become managers and leaders. How can anthropology teachers help prepare them for the real-life issues they are likely to face?

One way is to integrate case studies, monographs, and ethnographies from contemporary societies into the course material. Much of this material can come from the activities of practitioners working and consulting in the business world.

Going further, the collaboration between anthropology and the business world can help create internships and practicums for anthropology students to give them practical experience in the real world. For instance, one consulting firm routinely hires college students as summer interns. Depending on the need, their responsibilities range from general office "go-fer" to actually participating in ongoing projects. In all cases, interns get to experience life in a consulting firm first-hand while getting some exposure to business at the same time.

Finally, anthropology courses could be more enjoyable and beneficial if teaching methods were modified to reflect some of the principles of adult learning. Just as with training programs, the best academic course material can be made deadly by poor presentation. As we have seen, management consultants have developed new and creative delivery methods—for example, role plays and other experiential learning exercises; case study analysis; and facilitation rather than "expert" lecturing. Many of these are applicable to the college classroom and would greatly enhance the acceptance and retention of course material as well as the ability to apply it outside of the classroom.

Notes

[1]This was the topic of a recent issue of *Fortune* magazine entitled, "Managing Now for the 1990's" (26 September 1988).

[2]These technological innovations also impact on social relations, not always in positive ways. For example, Schein (1985:18) describes a situation where managers decided against using the new electronic mail system when they realized how important the "personal relations" aspect of face-to-face contact and frequent meetings were to getting the job done.

[3]For discussions of the functions of management see Fayol (1949) and Drucker (1974).

[4]This example comes from an educational film entitled, *Valuing Diversity* (Copeland, Griggs Production, 1988).

[5]Personal communication: Joann Baney, Director of Public Information, Association of Management.Consulting Firms, New York, NY.

[6]The cases we present are largely drawn from our experiences and the experiences of colleagues. Since neither of us has engaged in market research, this type of management consulting is not represented here. For information about what anthropologists are doing in marketing consulting, see Dickie (1982); Gardner (1978); Lewin (1986); and J. C. Louis (1985).

[7]Some businesses have applied this principle by creating opportunities for employees to spend time in other work or functional areas. In many cases, these efforts have improved intergroup communications. The same principle may be behind the Japanese practice of having managers rotate through different departments and functional areas during their careers so that they better understand the specific issues of each group as well as how the groups fit together.

[8]Originally developed by Flanagan (1954), the methods of critical event analysis were further refined and used extensively by McClelland (1976) in gathering data about motivation and competencies of high-performing individuals.

[9]Deal and Kennedy's *Corporate Culture* (1982) exemplifies the popular use of the culture concept. Some very good books and articles have been written about organizational culture (Frost et al. 1985; Kilmann et al. 1985; Pondy et al. 1983). But, for the most part, these are academic in nature and have not become popularized.

[10]Personal communication: Constance Perin.

References Cited

Adler, Nancy J.
1986 International Dimensions of Organizational Behavior. Boston: Kent Publishing Company.

Baba, Marietta
1988a Local Knowledge Systems in Advanced Technology Organizations. *In* Strategic Management in High Technology Firms. Gomez Meija, Luis Lawless and M. Lawless, eds. Greenwich, CT: JAI Press.
1988b Two Sides to Every Story: An Ethnohistorical Approach to Organizational Partnerships. City and Society 2(2):71–104.

Block, Peter
1981 Flawless Consulting. Austin: Learning Concepts.

Boston Globe
1988 Fighting Racism, Sexism at Work. August 21, pp. 63, 96.

Briggs, Charles
1986 Learning How to Ask. New York: Cambridge University Press.

Business Week
1989 Investing for the 1990's. October 16, pp. 91–102.

Chambers, Erve
1985 Applied Anthropology: A Practical Guide. New Jersey: Prentice-Hall.

Copeland, Griggs Production
1988 Valuing Diversity (film). Copeland, Griggs Productions. San Francisco, CA.

Deal, Terrence E., and Allen A. Kennedy
1982 Corporate Cultures, the Rites and Rituals of Corporate Life. Reading, MA: Addison Wesley.

Dickie, W.
1982 Profile of an Anthropologist: Anthropology in and of the Marketplace. Anthropology Newsletter 23(9):7.

Drucker, Peter
1974 Management: Tasks, Responsibilities, Practices. New York: Harper and Row.

Eddy, Elizabeth M., and W. L. Partridge, eds.
1978 Applied Anthropology in America. New York: Columbia University Press.

Fayol, Henri
1949[1917] General and Industrial Management. Constance Storrs, trans. London: Pitman.

Flanagan, J. C.
1954 The Critical Incident Technique. Psychological Bulletin 51(4):327–358.

Fortune Magazine
1980 New Management at Bendix. November 3, pp. 48–52.
1988 Managing Now for the 1990's (Special issue). September 26.
1989 Stars of the 1980's Cast Their Light. July 3, pp. 66–88.

Frost, Peter et al., eds
1985 Organizational Culture. Beverly Hills: Sage Publications.

Gamst, Frederick
1977 An Integrating View of the Underlying Premises of an Industrial Ethnology in the United States and Canada. Anthropological Quarterly 50:1–8.
1980 Toward a Method of Industrial Ethnology. Rice University Studies 66(1):15–42.

Gardner, B. B.
1978 Doing Business with Management. *In* Applied Anthropology in America. E. M. Eddy and W. L. Partridge, eds., pp. 245–260. New York: Columbia University Press.

Hanamura, Steve
1989 Working with People Who Are Different. Training and Development Journal 43(9):110–114.
Haynes, Arden
1989 What About the Future? Business Quarterly. Spring, pp. 54–57.
Holzberg, Carol, and Maureen Giovannini
1981 Anthropology and Industry: Reappraisal and New Directions. Annual Review of Anthropology 10:317–360.
Kilmann, Ralph, et al., eds.
1985 Gaining Control of the Corporate Culture. San Francisco: Jossy-Bass.
Kirk J., and M. L. Miller
1986 Reliability and Validity in Qualitative Research. Beverly Hills: Sage Publications.
Lewin, T.
1986 Casting An Anthropological Eye On American Consumers. New York Times. May 11, p. 6.
Louis, J. C.
1985 It's Anthropological: Research Takes a "Cultural Bent." Advertising Age. January 14, pp. 3, 31.
Louis, M. R.
1985 Sourcing Workplace Cultures: Why, When, and How. *In* Gaining Control of the Corporate Culture. R. Kilmann, et al. eds., pp. 126–136. San Francisco: Jossy-Bass.
McClelland, D. C.
1976 A Guide to Job Competence Assessment. Boston: McBur and Company.
Mead, Margaret
1970 Culture and Commitment. New York: The American Museum of Natural History.
Mintzberg, Henry
1984 The Manager's Job: Folklore and Fact. *In* Organization and People. J. B. Ritchie and P. Thompson, eds., pp. 276–292. St. Paul: West Publications.
Oshry, Barry
1982 Middles of the World, Integrate. Boston: Power & Systems Training, Inc.
Pelto, Pertie, and Gretel H. Pelto
1978 Anthropological Research: The Structure of Inquiry: Cambridge: Cambridge University Press.
Phatak, Arvind V.
1989 International Dimensions of Management (2nd edition). Boston: PWS-Kent Publishing Company.
Pondy, Louis R. et al., eds.
1983 Organizational Symbolism. Greenwich, Conn: JAI Press, Inc.
Prestowitz, Clyde Jr.
1988 Trading Places. New York: Basic Books.
Schein, Edgar
1969 Process Consultation: Its Role in Organizational Development. Reading, MA: Addison Wesley.
1985 How Culture Forms, Develops, and Changes. *In* Gaining Control of the Corporate Culture. Ralph Kilmann et al., eds., pp. 17–43. San Francisco: Jossy-Bass.
1987 The Clinical Perspective in Fieldwork. New Jersey: Sage Publications.
Taylor, F. W.
1911 The Principles of Scientific Management. New York: Harper.
Taylor, Natalie, and Lynne Rosansky
1988 What Managers Do. Waltham, MA: AMA Extension Institute.
Terpstra, V., and K. David
1985 The Cultural Environment of International Business (2nd edition). Cincinnati: SouthWestern Publishing Co.
Werner, Oswald, and Mark Schoepfle
1987 Ethnographic Analysis and Data Management (vol 2). Beverly Hills: Sage Publications.
Wilhite, Jim O.
1989 A Point of View: Toughness and True Leadership in the 1990's. National Productivity Review. 8(3):219–222.

Wolfe, Alvin
1977 The Supranational Organization of Production: An Evolutionary Perspective. Current Anthropology 18(4):615–635.
Zemke, Ron
1989 Anthropologists in the "Corporate Jungle." Training Magazine 26(4):49–60.

About the Authors

Maureen J. Giovannini is a cultural anthropologist employed by ODI, an international management consulting firm located in Burlington, Massachusetts. She received her MA and Ph.D. from Syracuse University and served on the faculty of Boston University from 1975 to 1986. Dr. Giovannini's academic work centered around industrialization and sociocultural change and the anthropology of health. She has published on these topics in several key journals including *The American Ethnologist, The Journal of the Royal Anthropological Institute, The American Anthropologist, Anthropology, and Social Science and Medicine.* Since joining ODI, Dr. Giovannini has consulted in the financial, healthcare, manufacturing, and service industries. She specializes in assessing the quality improvement needs of organizations and helping managers effect organizational change. Dr. Giovannini is currently involved in implementing quality improvement in different cultural contexts and recently delivered a paper on this subject at an international meeting.

Lynne M. H. Rosansky is an Assistant Professor of Management at Babson College, where she teaches General Management, The Manager and Society and Organizational Behavior. She received her Ph.D. in Cultural Anthropology from Boston University in 1984 and her MBA from Babson College in 1989. Her most recent research and publication was in the area of international competitive strategy. Other areas of interest include business ethics, leadership and organizational change. She co-authored *What Managers Do,* with Natalie Taylor in 1988. Dr. Rosansky has been a practicing management consultant since 1980. Her consulting work has focused on leadership issues, performance management and organizational change. Her clients have included large Fortune 100 companies, hospitals, and government managers as well as small businesses.